A Book of Spiritual Wisdom
☼ for all days ☾

Marijo Moore

rENEGADE pLANETS pUBLISHING

rENEGADE pLANETS pUBLISHING
PO Box 2493
Candler, NC 28715
renegadepl@aol.com
First Edition

Library of Congress Control Number: 2011921751
ISBN: 978-0-9767581-6-7

Layout, cover and interior design by baddog creative–baddogcreative.com

Cover art: "Of Spirits and the Universe," © 2010 MariJo Moore, mixed media collage, 4 ¾" x 6." Poem on back cover "Energy Never Ends: On Being A Medium" ©2010 MariJo Moore

Drawings of the Author by Ms. Moore's granddaughters, Zoey Makayla Jaynes, age 9, and Emma Kate Jaynes, age 6. ©2011 ZMJ and EKJ, pen and ink collage, 5" by 8"

Contents

March 21

Week One   *Seek your answers inside your own heart. Time has come to stop searching for the opinions of others on matters of your spiritual growth.*

Week Two   *What you seek in love is not only in your soul. It also lies sleeping in the souls of others. Awaken it with prayer.*

Week Three   *Some days you get the bear. Some days the bear gets you. And some days, you can't even find the woods.*

Week Four   *You know it is time for a change whenever anger at yourself swells inside causing your heart to hurt.*

April 31

Week One   *Try saying no when you are tempted to say yes and see how your life changes focus.*

Week Two   *When the area around you is shaking, look to see what you are standing on.*

Week Three   *An optional reproductive decision for some can be a brutal reality for others.*

Week Four   *Romance can and does exist outside of books.*

May 41

Week One	*The color of one's skin cannot determine how fragile is a heart.*
Week Two	*Consider the fact that all our parents were young people before becoming our mothers and fathers. Then rethink judging their life choices.*
Week Three	*To question your motives is the timeliest gift you can give yourself.*
Week Four	*Moon time is a way of evolving and releasing knowledge you no longer need, or do not understand.*

June 51

Week One	*Many years ago, in most Indigenous nations, when decisions concerning the environment were made, the effect these decisions would have on seven generations was the highest consideration.*
Week Two	*Remember to give thanks for all blessings and do not feign unhappiness over things that have not yet reached their times of manifestation.*
Week Three	*Long times of rest are important when one continues searching in spiritual matters.*
Week Four	*Gathering corn is often not as important as gathering seeds.*

July

Week One   *Spirituality and creativity are deeply connected in children.*

Week Two   *There are so many things we can inherit from our ancestors: eye color, hair color, body frame, finger length, innate talents, creativity, et cetera. We can also inherit one of life's major challenges: Addiction.*

Week Three   *You are a sacred stone on which meaningful carvings are being added daily.*

Week Four   *Direct all healing energy with thoughtful prayer.*

August

Week One   *The purpose of ceremony is to integrate: to unite one with all of humankind as well as the realm of the ancestors, to blend one with all of creation.*

Week Two   *Forgiveness of yourself does not mean forgetting, but getting on with your life.*

Week Three   *Death is never without purpose.*

Week Four   *Is it true that time heals all wounds, or if we let enough time pass, we learn to accept the ambivalent nature of others?*

September 81

Week One   *Sacrifice cleanses the spirit.*

Week Two   *Look underneath the dry hostility to find the painful truths.*

Week Three   *Whatever you feel is dragging you down is simply trying to get your attention.*

Week Four   *What is war? How can we define this frightening word?*

October 91

Week One   *Some cannot deal with all their fears and regretful actions in this realm. Instead they take the most painful ones to the other realm and work to understand them there.*

Week Two   *The Universal Soul speaks in silence.*

Week Three   *Creativity is a gift from Spirit to all humans.*

Week Four   *There is no magic in Spiritual medicine, or in being a Spiritual healer. How does anyone deal with such responsibility? There is no right or wrong answer, simply this question that melts away from the healer's consciousness as he or she becomes fully accepting of the accountability.*

November 101

Week One *Light brings destruction to what has lived inside the darkness for too, too long.*

Week Two *Grief of losing a love one can stay within us for years. Learning how to deal with it can be the answer to moving toward acceptance.*

Week Three *Crows are our buddies.*

Week Four *Spirit beings are all around us.*

December 111

Week One *You've struggled far too long over empty nests. When one is empty, take apart and begin anew.*

Week Two *Whatever the next story is in your life, it will come to you; it will find you.*

Week Three *You are strong only when you can recognize and accept your weaknesses so that they may not be used against you.*

Week Four *The mysteries remain awaiting appreciation.*

About the Author 121

Drawings of the Author 123

To Continuing Existence...

Introduction

The entries* in this compilation are based upon spiritual intuitive consultations from the past twenty years. I am gifted with spiritual insight, the ability to be a "medium" for those who have passed over, and have had the opportunity to work with many people who have come to me to ask for guidance, spiritual support, and to contact their loved ones. Though it is impossible for any spiritual medium to claim accuracy a hundred percent of the time, I am blessed with a gift strong enough to be able to be used by Spirit** to help others in times of need.

Some of the subjects in these entries were once considered "taboo to discuss." That time has passed. We are now in a spiritual shift where we must deal with everything that has happened to us, consider the possibilities of future happenings, and glean wisdom from these to help us continue to thrive in our spiritual progress on this planet.

I do not claim to be an expert on any one subject. I do not claim to be anything other than who I am: a woman who has the uncanny ability to listen to the other side and bring forth messages. I give credit to Spirit for this gift, and for allowing me to be a vessel.

Although broken at times, I am willing to keep going forward during the mending.

The quotes at the beginning of each entry are from my collective writings – some old, some new. My objective is to help those who can be helped with these insights. Again, I thank Spirit for allowing me to share.

MariJo Moore, 2011

In the mountains of western North Carolina

* Please note there are four weekly entries for each of the twelve months. I am aware that some months sometimes have five weeks, but in order to use this book during any year, I suggest during the months with five weeks, you choose one of the four entries and use it for two weeks.

** Spirit is used synonymously with God, Creator, Universe and All There Is.

January February

March April

May June

July August

September October

November December

Week One

Truth is what lives on eternally despite all the lies holding this world together.

Why do people lie? I have lied, you have lied, everyone we know has lied at one time or another. But why? Does lying about our accomplishments cover low self-esteem? Are we afraid if we tell the truth we will be punished, or perhaps denied something we think we deserve? Where do lies come from? What about truth? Why do we tell the truth when we know we could get by with a lie?

We humans are complex beings. Our reasoning and spirit are constantly in conflict and constantly wanting to become balanced on an equal scale of living that just might not exist.

If you are struggling with truth and its opposite, lying, you are not alone. Many others are experiencing the same conundrum at this precise time. Ask yourself if you would rather deal with the consequences/aftermath of telling the truth or a lie. Ask yourself if you had rather be told the truth or a lie. Then make your decision.

One thing is for certain, however. The truth will come out. Maybe not today. Maybe not tomorrow. Maybe not until the next century. But truth is going to expose itself, in one form or another. Always.

Meanwhile, stay strong.

Notes ☼ Thoughts ☾ Prayers

Week Two

Spirituality is paying attention.

There is no perfect way to describe or define spirituality. Regardless of which religion you may honor, or even if you don't indulge in religion, spirituality has different connotations to all of us.

Why? Because spirituality develops more deeply from experience than from any other form of knowledge. We can learn about spirituality from teachings, reading books, or listening to others. But to truly develop our own spiritually, we have to consider what we have experienced, not just what others share with us.

Spirituality is a highly private affair, because even though we are all One, we are all an essential part of this One. We may be alike in many ways, but we are each unique in how we spiritualize our experiences of life. How we digest them, view them, honor them, hate them, love them, learn from them, ignore them, et cetera.

Take some time to think about an upcoming opportunity you can experience in a spiritual fashion. Try to see the workings of Spirit in this situation. Then, give thanks for having the opportunity to be an important component in the wholeness of the One.

Do you doubt your importance? Don't.
Stay strong.

Notes ☼ Thoughts ☾ Prayers

Week Three

There is no distance between dreams and reality.

A dream can be a subconscious cleansing.
Sometimes there are hurts so painful conscious minds cannot support them. They are buried deep within the subconscious and dreams can help clear them out. Measure the importance of your cleansing dreams by how quickly you forget them.
A dream can be a deepening voyage.
We often travel to visit with ancestral spirits, the spirits of loved ones who have passed over, and the spirits of descendants to come. If we are not able to make these visits in waking lives, a dream can take us on these important voyages.
A dream can be an enlightening glimpse.
If we are undecided about which path to take, which decision to make, which person to love, which person to leave behind, which job to take, and so forth, a dream can give us an enlightening glimpse into what is best for us in all manner of life, giving our spirits the strength we need to carry on.
Dreams come when we most need them.

Continue to dream.
Stay strong.

Notes ☼ Thoughts ☾ Prayers

Week Four

Songs can lighten the world,
but can also bring up dark memories.

Think of a song you used to listen to again and again. Think of the words, the tune, and the significance of them in your life during this time. Do old feelings resurface? Do you feel uneasy because of decisions made? Are you melancholy for someone or something? Do the words dredge up memories you would like to change? All of these feelings are normal. We are creatures of habit. Often we connect songs with feelings, emotional memories, and doubtful times in our lives.

Give yourself permission to give yourself new memories. Play the song – either in reality or in your imagination – and retrain your thoughts to think on good things, good times, and the best of the situation. Say a prayer for upliftment for all involved with any dark memories and allow yourself to gather strength from this prayer. As you pray for another, you are also praying for yourself.

The next time you think of this song, the next time you awake with it on your mind, the next time it visits your dreams, the next time you hear it playing, remind yourself: You have prayed for all involved with the dark memories and therefore the song can only become a hauntingly beautiful reminder for you of how far you have come.

Sing often. Stay strong.

Notes ☀ Thoughts ☾ Prayers

January **February**

March April

May June

July August

September October

November December

Week One

Money comes, money goes, and money comes again.

What is money and why do we concern ourselves with it so often? If it is energy, like everything else in our world, why can we not just "call it into existence"? Whether we grew up in poverty or riches, whether we accept the societal ideology of how money controls our world, whether we have plenty or not enough or just enough to get by, money is one aspect of our lives that can cause sleepless nights, arguments with loved ones, the ending of friendships, the dubious adoration of others, or the miscalculated judgment of others.

Bartering is one way we can lessen money worries. But it is not possible to barter necessities like electricity and other modern conveniences we have come to depend on. And if we don't pay these bills, these modern conveniences can quickly become things of the past.

So, should we work harder, keep borrowing, keep giving, keep hoping, or just give up? Each situation has to be handled individually concerning the person's beliefs, trust in others as well as in oneself, the ability to ask for help when needed, to share what one is given, and to realize that absolutely nothing is guaranteed in this life. Therefore it is better not to depend upon any certainty other than life will use your wants and insecurities to teach you your most valuable lessons.

Accept what comes and bless what goes. Stay strong.

Notes ☀ Thoughts ☾ Prayers

Week Two

*There is much to be said for the healing power of words - the
medium of mystics, prophets, and healers for thousands of years.*

Many of us have had heard how words from a movie, poem,
song, or book saved a life; how the overheard words of
strangers gave someone hope, clarity, or guidance. How words
of inspiration and creativity were whispered into people's ears
from invisible sources. How the words they needed to hear
came at exactly the precise times they needed to hear them.

Are we paying attention to what words fill our lives daily? Are we
trying to be positive in our words to others, but most importantly,
to ourselves? Words can have healing power, but words can also
wound deeply. Be mindful of the words you say and the way
you say them. Inflection can change one's whole outlook on a
situation. The intent behind words is where the power resides.

There is an American Indian oral tradition in which words
function as a part of the healing process by transformation and
restoration. This tradition can be practiced through the written
as well as the spoken word. Write a note telling yourself how
deserving of a wonderful life you are. Put this note where you
can see it. Read these words aloud every day. Read them again
and again and again until you begin to believe them. Share
your thoughts with others and encourage them to write.

Then read the words again. Stay strong.

Notes ☀ Thoughts ☾ Prayers

Week Three

There is no way humans can fully understand the strength and determination of love. Only when we pass on to another realm will we be able to begin to fully grasp what powerful energy love is.

Love can be the most stagnant and most moving of all energies. We often block it in this realm by layering it with restrictions: "If you love me, you'll do this. If you love me, you won't do this," et cetera. This is not love. This is an exploitation of love. Remember, energy reforms itself repeatedly. We can block it with our human desires, but we can also get a deeper understanding of this energy by trying to love ourselves so we can be more accepting of others.

But to actually love oneself is to accept all of oneself, and in order to truly accept all of oneself, we have to understand the reasoning behind all happenings and circumstances concerning us. This is not humanly possible, so the paramount we can hope for is to be easy on ourselves, forgive ourselves, and accept the fact we are spiritual beings experiencing human lives. A large part of our spiritual path is continuing to try to know ourselves on a deeper level. There are many ways to do this - therapy, gatherings, meditation, creativity, teaching, learning, sharing, giving, receiving, et cetera. We have to seek which method or methods work best at this time for each of us, and continue to try and love ourselves the best we can.

Know that we all have an essential place in this realm.
Stay strong.

Notes ☀ Thoughts ☾ Prayers

Week Four

Except in times of deep, deep darkness, do not pray for a way out. Hard work strengthens your determination.

Ever think you should just give up on a project? Let go of a dream you have been trying to nurture for years? Turn your back on someone who tends to wallow in misery instead of stepping up and taking charge of his/her life? Stop giving so much when receiving nothing in return? One spiritual law that tends to show itself time and again is that you get back what you give eventually, but not necessarily from the person to whom you gave.

Think back on something in your life that you thought you could never accomplish but eventually did. Someone you thought you could never help but did. Now think of how your determination was strengthened by these episodes. Learning that nothing in this realm is really free – that everything we receive comes with either hard work or a sacrifice of some kind - is something we need to remember every day. But if the situation or person you are struggling with brings a draining darkness into your life, then pray for Spirit to give you a way out that is good for all concerned. We cannot help those who refuse to help themselves. They can only bring us down to their level.

Determination is the key to accomplishing goals, but sometimes the hardest thing to do is to do nothing and let Spirit take over.

In the intervening time, stay strong.

Notes ☼ Thoughts ☾ Prayers

January February

March April

May June

July August

September October

November December

Week One

Seek your answers inside your own heart. Time has come to stop searching for the opinions of others on matters of your spiritual growth.

There can be no generalization concerning one person's spiritual growth because we are whom we are due to DNA, genetic memory, experiences, past and future lives. If there is something we know we should not do – if we are asking a question we already know the answer to, hoping to hear someone else tell us what we want to hear - then we are fooling ourselves. If we receive confirmation of what we know the right answer to be, that is a different matter.

You can always find someone - if you continue asking for the opinions of others – who will tell you what you think you want to hear. If this works for you, then by all means, keep on until you find someone to agree with you and then act against your intuition. Just be ready to suffer the consequences.

Many people go to seer after seer, psychic after psychic, medium after medium, friend after friend, enemy after enemy until they hear what they think they want to hear, when all along they already hold the answer in their hearts. There can be many answers to every spiritual question. Choose the one that you know is right for you.

In to one tiny moment any answer can come if you are paying attention, and can only remember what you have asked.

Trust yourself. Stay Strong.

Notes ☀ Thoughts ☾ Prayers

Week Two

*What you seek in love is not only in your soul. It also lies
sleeping in the souls of others. Awaken it with prayer.*

If you feel there is no love in your life, or there isn't enough love
in your life, you are the responsible party. You hold in you all
the love anyone could ever experience – you just have to give it
permission to reach out to others.

There are many forms of human love and many ways to love. So-
called brotherly love (which encompasses family, acquaintances,
neighbors, and so forth) is not always an easy task. Some people
we have to love from a distance, just as some people decide to love
us from a distance. There are some people in our lives that we are
not able to love, no matter how much we want to, no matter how
hard we try. The best we can do for them and for ourselves is to
pray they are given health, prosperity and happiness.

Romantic love is fickle. There are those with whom we would
like to give our love but do not want to accept it. And there
are those who would like us to love them romantically but we
choose not to. Again, we must pray and ask for guidance in this
matter. What will be will be. The results are left up to Spirit.

Every person on this earth has love sleeping deeply inside his/
her soul. We do not know exactly what human love is, but we
can be sure of one thing: Love often presents itself as respect.

Respect yourself and others. Stay strong.

Notes ☼ Thoughts ☾ Prayers

Week Three

Some days you get the bear. Some days the bear gets you.
And some days, you can't even find the woods.

What a day! You are either too cold or too hot. Too busy or too bored. Too this or too that. Take a second, take a deep breath, and relax. Just how important is the subject you are worrying about? Just how important is it that you look perfect? Just how important is it that everything goes your way?

Instead of trying to make sense of a day like this, get on with your life by being grateful for all that has come to you lately. Did you have a nice place to sleep last night? If so, be grateful. If not, ask for one for tonight. Did you have enough to eat yesterday? If yes, be grateful. If not, ask for help.

Is there at least one person you can call and say, "I am thinking of you and wish you the best?" Then do it. If not, then rethink your relationships.

Life goes on. We are remarkably successful some days, we seem to accomplish nothing some days, and some days we just need to sit down and be grateful. Let what will be just be. We all have days we wish we could start over and we can. At any time, we can start our day anew. Remember this and take advantage of it whenever you need to. Accept things where they are, then venture forward.

Again, take a deep breath, relax, and smile. Stay strong.

Notes ☀ Thoughts ☾ Prayers

Week Four

You know it is time for a change whenever anger at yourself swells inside causing your heart to hurt.

If we are hurting inside, aching because we feel we don't have the right to correct a situation, because we don't have the guts to speak up about something, because we are afraid of someone, because we don't think we deserve the best, deserve to be happy, then that hurt is caused by anger. Anger towards oneself.

No doubt it is time to sit down and write a letter to yourself. Spill out all the anger and frustration and get to the bottom of why you are so angry with yourself. Ask yourself questions and answer them to the best of your ability. Then wait a while, go back to the letter and answer the questions again. This time let the hurt out alongside the anger. Cleanse yourself of all the contempt you feel toward yourself. Read between the lines and fill in the gaps where you know you are not being honest with yourself.

Read this letter aloud to yourself. Cry, scream, laugh, and hit a pillow, then cry some more if need be. Then, burn this letter. You will feel a bit exhausted but so much lighter once you do this. Seek outside help if you feel you need it. Love yourself enough to take care of yourself. You're doing better and better every day! And remember, depression can be anger turned inward.

Do something nice for yourself. Stay strong.

Notes ☀ Thoughts ☾ Prayers

January February

March **April**

May June

July August

September October

November December

31

Week One

Try saying no when you are tempted to say yes and see how your life changes focus.

Sometimes we have a hard time saying no when we know we should. Why? Perhaps we don't want to start an argument. Possibly we think we can change our minds later on and say no then. Probably we don't want to suffer the consequences if we don't agree. Maybe we are afraid we won't be liked, accepted, asked again, et cetera.

Saying yes when we know we should say no causes us to become dissatisfied with ourselves. It can cause us to do things that we really do not want to do, cause us manifest frustrations and on and on. This can turn into a habit that taints your personal decisions concerning what is good for you and what is not.

It is time we learn to say no when we need to. Keep a watchful eye on yourself and see if you do say yes when you want to say no. Have the courage to say no and then see how good you feel about yourself. The more we say no to what we do not want in our lives, the stronger we become and the more enjoyable our lives turn out to be. Every time you say no, it becomes easier to say no the next time.

Learn to say no to what you don't want in your life.
Stay strong.

Notes ☼ Thoughts ☾ Prayers

Week Two

When the area around you is shaking,
look to see what you are standing on.

Feeling like the world is out to get you? Nothing seems to be going your way? Do you feel like running and hiding and ignoring all responsibilities?

Where is your faith? What/Who do you put your faith in? Have you lost touch with your source of guidance? Your source of encouragement?

What are you standing on? Lies? Promises? Second Guesses? Where has your version of truth gone? Can you rise above the shaky time? Can you learn to live with it or walk away?

Time to sit down and take a closer look at what you have built your life upon. Time to take some time off and consider where you are being spiritually fed. Time to recollect any times in your life that have been as shaky or shakier than now. How did you mange to survive those? What kept you going? What gave you strength?

Life continues on whether we are paying attention or not, whether we are considerate of our surroundings or not, whether we seek clarity or not. Be prepared by finding your solid center upon which to stand.

Look around; take notice of everything in your life.
Stay strong.

Notes ☀ Thoughts ☾ Prayers

Week Three

*An optional reproductive decision for some
can be a brutal reality for others.*

Those of us who are fertile have the option to become sterile to prevent birth. Whether done for medical, emotional, financial or other reasons, it is most likely a personal choice. We can make this choice, have the process done, and we have the option of having the situation reversed.

However, it is a fact that many people have been, and continue to be, forcibly sterilized by government mandate. All over the world this atrocity has happened and continues to happen. Many people are not even told they are being sterilized until after the fact. Consider that numerous American Indian women were sterilized without their consent in the 1960-70s. Consider the Third Reich's sterilization law. And these are just two instances. Regardless of what unjust reasoning (eugenics, propaganda, racism, religious control) behind this act, forced sterilization has distressed the lives of millions, and is still happening worldwide even as you read this. Reflect on what has happened to these people and what continues to happen. What can you do? Write letters? Post your objections on websites? Why not pray? Say a prayer for those who have undergone and are undergoing this transgression. Pray they have strength to go forward and maintain their dignity. And pray for those wanting fertility as well.

*Stay strong so you can pray for those
who need your strong prayers.*

Notes ☼ Thoughts ☾ Prayers

Week Four

Romance can and does exist outside of books.

Were you taught to be romantic? Most of us were not. Instead we grew up thinking romance consists of taking all the abuse someone can muster, and then forgiving him or her enough to crawl back into bed. We obviously saw sex confused with romance. Gifts confused with sex. Sex confused with threats. Threats confused with love, and so we are mostly confused about what romance really is. Period.

To some of us who endured childhood pain, we waited on that wonderful knight on a white horse to come and save us. Even if he or she showed up in a broken down Pinto, we ran off with the driver, hoping to find love outside the situation we had to endure.

Can romance exist outside those novels with covers of gorgeous unrealistic hunks and women who look as though they have never endured a broken nail, much less a broken heart? Would we recognize romance if it showed up in our lives, clad in a bouquet of roses and smelling like forever? Possibly not. It seems we can read about it, but not trust it. And even if we have experienced something close to romance, we often talk ourselves out of it. Again, we just don't seem to trust that life can be good for us; that we are romance worthy. But it can and we are. We just have to accept that romance can live outside books and inside hearts.

Think romantic thoughts. Stay strong.

Notes ☀ Thoughts ☾ Prayers

January February

March April

May June

July August

September October

November December

Week One

*The color of one's skin cannot determine
how fragile is a heart.*

We have all experienced racism in one form or another, either being the target, instigator, or witness. Buried within all of our psyches is the human belief that we all need someone to look down on to make us feel better about ourselves. Doesn't matter if you were not raised to be racist, doesn't matter if you don't have any problems with other races; this is a belief that has been in our psyches since time immemorial. And this belief shows itself when we least expect it.

If you were in an elevator full of people and the only one of your race, what thoughts would you have? If your son, daughter, sister, brother, or anyone in your family fell in love with someone not of your race, how would you react? Life gives us opportunity after opportunity to test our beliefs concerning others. But aren't we all possibly the same inside, regardless of skin color? Can hurt be less painful because of another's race? Of course not.

We should look into our hearts and see if we are indeed looking down on others, and if we are, ask ourselves why. Isn't it time we concentrate on the similarities we share instead of the differences? To realize we are all part of the whole? This just might be the answer to stopping some of the hate in this world.

*Think of others of different races and
send good thoughts to them. Stay strong.*

Notes ☀ Thoughts ☾ Prayers

Week Two

Consider the fact that all our parents were young people before becoming our mothers and fathers. Then rethink judging their life choices.

There is no way we will ever entirely know the lives our parents had before we were born. Their childhood heartbreaks and happy times, their struggles with their parents, grandparents, teachers, their relationships, abuse, whatever.

If we can think of our parents as human beings, not saviors, if we can look at our own lives and realize how long it has taken (or is taking) us to learn to parent, then maybe we can be a bit more tolerant.

There are parents who abandon their children, kill them, abuse them sexually, physically, emotionally, and mentally. This is a given fact. But there are also parents who care for their children, who make sacrifices, stand up for them, and give them everything they need. There are mothers and fathers who, in later years, seek to mend relationships with themselves so that they can mend relationships with others. But sadly, many do not. We have to realize our mothers and fathers once lived in a different world than we do today. They did not have the opportunities to seek help as we do. And even if offered help, many were and are too afraid or stubborn to ask.

Think of your parents, whether alive or in spirit, in good terms. Stay strong.

Notes ☼ Thoughts ☾ Prayers

Week Three

To question your motives is the
timeliest gift you can give yourself.

What do you have planned for today? For this week? Have you stopped to think about why you are going to do the things you have planned?

Do you plan on giving away something that you no longer use? Why? To get rid of it, to clear out space so something better can come into your life, or to gift someone with something you know they would like to have?

Are you going to visit a family member? Why? Because you really want to see this person, or because you feel obligated to visit? Are you going to call instead of visit in person? If it is not possible to visit in person, are you still going to call? Write a letter? Send a note?

Do you plan on buying something nice for yourself? Why? Because you think you deserve it? Because it makes you feel better? Because no one else will? Because you love yourself?

Do you plan to do something you have been putting off for a while, or are you going to make more excuses not to do it? Why? Do you fear the outcome? Do you fear you are not doing the right thing? Are you afraid of being judged, maybe not getting the credit you feel you merit?

Give yourself the gift of considering your motives.
Stay strong.

Notes ☀ Thoughts ☾ Prayers

Week Four

Moon time is a way of evolving and releasing knowledge you no longer need, or do not understand.

How often have you complained about moon time? Your period? Your monthly visitor? Or whatever you were taught to call your menstruation. Cramps, excessive bleeding, irritability, and the ultimate need to just "be left alone," often accompany those who dread this cycle. But this is a time of cleansing, a time to let go of what you do not need or cannot yet understand, and a time to evolve into becoming stronger in your feminine power.

Menstrual taboos are about power, not sin or filth. In several Indigenous nations, women who are at the peak of their fecundity are believed to possess power that totally throws male power out of kilter. A feminine power in the sense of a greater connection to the Spirit of All There Is – a connection that gives them an open door to the universe. Therefore any "male-owned or dominated ritual or sacred object" cannot perform its usual task and that is why women are kept from them during their cycles.

As we grow older and our cycles stop altogether, this is when we retain the wisdom of our feminine ancestral blood that we need to become elders. Spirit uses our bodies to cleanse our thoughts and prepare us to help others in many ways.

Be grateful that feminine power flows through your veins. Stay strong.

Notes ☀ Thoughts ☾ Prayers

January February
March April
May June
July August
September October
November December

Week One

Many years ago, in most Indigenous nations, when decisions concerning the environment were made, the effect these decisions would have on seven generations was the highest consideration.

Seven generations: you, your children, grandchildren, great grand children, great great grandchildren, great great great grandchildren, and great great great great grandchildren. Wouldn't it be nice to know that when decisions concerning the environment are made today, this would also be the most important consideration? Not one of us can live without clean water or oxygen. Sooner or later, if the pollution and rape of this planet keeps going at the rate it has for the past one hundred years, this may be a problem we have to face.

The acceptance that we are not in control of but dependent upon nature for our existence is a stark reality. So many people want technology to offer its quick fixes without taking adequate time to explore the mystery of spiritual interconnectedness. The true meaning of life can only be determined by realizing how everything in nature is interdependent, not by deciding what people, animals, minerals or plants we can do without. And if we are using up all our natural resources now, what will be left by the time our seventh generations arrive? Perhaps tempering modern technology with spiritual wisdom should be the ultimate quest.

Think of ways you can help the next seven generations.
Stay strong.

Notes ☀ Thoughts ☾ Prayers

Week Two

*Remember to give thanks for all blessings and
do not feign unhappiness over things that have not yet
reached their times of manifestation.*

Impatience is something we can all relate to. When we want something to happen, we want it to happen now! When we want someone to be with us, we want him or her to be with us now! When we want a job promotion, raise, transfer, new house, new car, or whatever, we want it now! But Spirit often has other plans.

Has there been a time in your life when you were disappointed when you didn't get what you wanted at the time you wanted it? Looking back, can you see that you might have settled for something far less than what Spirit had planned for you if you had gotten your way? Think of the blessing that came instead and be grateful.

We can't always know what is best for us or when something is supposed to manifest for us. Faith comes into the equation when we realize there is a much Higher Power than our wants. A Higher Power that knows what is best for us.

Time is an illusion dancing only within your mind. Timing is everything.

*Give thanks whenever you receive blessings.
Stay strong.*

Notes ☀ Thoughts ☾ Prayers

Week Three

Long times of rest are important when one continues searching in spiritual matters.

We often push ourselves to the limit with our spiritual searching. We meditate, walk labyrinths, seek answers in prayer, attend church, attend ceremonies, read self-help books, honor medicine wheels, help others, and on and on. If we aren't doing these as much as possible, then we sometimes feel guilty because we don't. But who says we have to be 100% spiritual ALL the time? Give yourself a break and yell a cuss word or two or three. Don't worry, lightning will not strike you. Tell Spirit how disappointed you are about something. How someone is getting on your nerves. How you are so tired of biting your tongue just to be nice. Go ahead. Say all this aloud to Spirit. Take the power out of it by saying it aloud. And again, don't worry. Spirit is stronger and larger than you can ever imagine, so you won't hurt Spirit's feelings or get in trouble.

Now, after you have done this, sit down and have a quiet laugh. Laugh at yourself for being so serious all the time. Lighten up. Enjoy the rest from being a "perfect spiritual being." Remember to occasionally take the time to unload your anger, distress, and just plain dissatisfaction. Spirit can take it.

Be human.
Stay strong.

Notes ☀ Thoughts ☾ Prayers

Week Four

Gathering corn is often not as important as gathering seeds.

Aging is something we have to deal with on a daily basis. When younger, we wanted to be older; now that we are growing older, we think of looking younger. Some of us age gracefully; some of us fight it all the way. Regardless, we are growing older and now is the time to consider what we can share with others.

Have you written the book you always wanted to write? Traveled to a special place? Accomplished what you have always wanted to accomplish? If not, then make a determined effort to begin. If money is not available for travel, then make a collage of places you would like to visit. Not as exciting as actual travel, of course, but still fun.

Life gives us beauty to absorb into our faces if we concentrate on gathering seeds to share with others. Maybe you won't be able to see it, but others will. Worried about gray hair? Either accept it or dye it. Hooded eyelids? Pretend you are a rattlesnake. Sagging in places? Exercise if you can or stop complaining. Why not enjoy what you have been given? There are people in this world who would love to have the problem of sagging weight.

You've gathered your corn through the years; now share the seeds of wisdom, laughter, love, creativity, and gratitude. And love yourself so that others can do the same.

Keep shucking. Stay strong.

Notes ☀ Thoughts ☾ Prayers

January February
March April
May June

July August

September October

November December

Week One

Spirituality and creativity are deeply connected in children.

This connection needs to be fed if children are to believe they have a place in this world. Helping young people understand their connection to the earth is extremely important. Inspiring them to produce creative works through that spiritual connection can become one of our greatest joys in life. (See page 123.)

Our bodies are connected to the earth, both physically and spiritually. At the most basic level, everything is created, lives, dies and returns to the earth to nourish things to come. Before European contact, aboriginal people had definite forms of education for children that were passed down from generation to generation, and all were centered on contact with the natural world. At our best we are connected to the animals, plants, rocks, the earth, and their voices and energy can speak to all of us. Understanding our connection with nature brings an understanding of our connection with all things.

Children know innately when they touch a tree or hold a flower that something inside them is going to click. If we can instill in children that they are part of the whole-a part of everything-they won't be as likely to abuse the land, each other or themselves. They will realize whatever they do effects so many other people. Children need opportunities to express themselves to reiterate this realization.

Give a child the occasion to express him or herself. Stay strong.

Notes ☀ Thoughts ☾ Prayers

Week Two

There are so many things we can inherit from our ancestors: eye color, hair color, body frame, finger length, innate talents, creativity, et cetera. We can also inherit one of life's major challenges: Addiction.

Odds are there is at least one, if not more, alcoholic and/or drug addict in your family. Perhaps you have an addiction problem and need to seek help. Or maybe you are in recovery. If so, then you know the pain, misery, and disruption any type of addiction can cause, the hell it can wreak on a family. And how it is often passed on from one generation to another.

We often hear of addiction-induced suicides (especially among youth), and the ever-present mental, physical, emotional and spiritual damages caused by alcoholism and drug abuse. Countless children are born addicted and with Fetal Alcohol Syndrome. Old and young suffer from addictions daily.

There is help available in so many forms that everyone should be able to find a way out of the hell of addiction. But there are those who do not get help, either because of choice, or because the addiction is stronger than they realize. Not all addict/alcoholics recover, not all stay in recovery.

It is your responsibility to let your children and grandchildren know what they may have inherited. Give them the education you may not have received. Give them what they deserve.

Share your truth. Stay strong.

Notes ☼ Thoughts ☾ Prayers

Week Three

You are a sacred stone on which
meaningful carvings are added daily.

Our lives consist of experiences, memories, gifts, loves, hates, delights, sorrows, wonderments, pains, fears, beliefs, disbeliefs, blessings, disappointments, lies, truths, work, play, stamina, exhaustion, creativity, destruction, and awareness of our senses being pushed to their limits. Are we paying attention to all aspects of our lives?

Everything, every person, every thought, every creation, every joy, every disappointment we experience are all carved into our spirits. We often don't slow down long enough to realize just what strong, wonderful beings we are. It is time we look at ourselves as sacred stones on which life carves meaning every day.

Do you ever stop and think how fortunate you are to be alive in this day and time? When a spiritual shift that is bringing masculine and feminine energies into alignment is going on inside us, as well as all around us? Balance is the key to feeling blessed. Let others know what you have survived, and give yourself credit for thriving. Let anger, resentment, disappointment and hurt rest for a week and see what comes your way. Emotional pain can be as devitalizing as physical pain.

Think good thoughts about yourself and toward others.
Stay strong.

Notes ☀ Thoughts ☾ Prayers

Week Four

Direct all healing energy with thoughtful prayer.

All of us, regardless of our walks in life, can be of healing help to those Spirit puts in our path who are hurting either emotionally, spiritually, mentally or physically. Spiritual Prayer is our connection to the whole. Pray to whatever deity you choose, just know that prayer is powerful and sets off healing energy. All is energy and the movement of energy connects all. You are an intermediary for energy and your thoughts and prayers can be deterrents or healants.

Always pray in specific wording. Think about what you are saying. If you do not know what to pray for, ask the person what he or she needs. When praying for another to heal from a specific disease or pain or emotional hurt, et cetera, be sure to ask for it to be taken away from the person and put into another realm so that it can be cleansed and come back as good for the person. Otherwise you will take on the pain, disease, et cetera. This is why so many who work with specific diseases get these same diseases.

We manifest what we dwell on. We are not totally responsible for all the thoughts that come into our minds, but we are responsible for those we let stay there and take root. Bad thoughts can come to fruition as easily as good thoughts. This does not mean you have total control over what happens but that you can draw to you what you think.

Be mindful of your thoughts and prayers. Stay strong.

Notes ☀ Thoughts ☾ Prayers

January February
March April
May June
July **August**
September October
November December

Week One

The purpose of ceremony is to integrate; to unite one
with all of humankind as well as the realm of
the ancestors, to blend one with all of creation.

Ceremony is a necessary act to obtain or regain balance with the universe. This allows us to raise consciousness and shed the idea of individuality. All ceremony brings us to the realization there is no separation from anything or anyone, provides great illumination, and gives us perception of a cosmic relationship. Only in isolation can sickness exist, therefore to heal, we must recognize oneness with the universe. This is spiritual medicine.

Each ceremony has its own special purpose. You can perform your own personal ceremony and show Spirit you are asking for help in becoming more balanced in your life.

There are not always instantaneous results of ceremonial rites. Therefore, we should not put more emphasis on the results than the actual ceremony. Timing is everything and timing consists of patience and shaping. Never use a ceremony to try and control another's actions. Never repeat the same ceremony over and over, trying to get results you desire. This shows a lack of faith and an unwillingness to be shaped by Spirit. Make sure you are willing to go through whatever Spirit designs to receive what you are asking for.

Turn your desires and needs over to Spirit and
leave the outcome to Universal wisdom that works
for the good of the whole. Stay strong.

Notes ☼ Thoughts ☾ Prayers

Week Two

Forgiveness of yourself does not mean forgetting,
but getting on with your life.

We've all done things, made decisions, ran away from, or ran toward things/people/places we wish we hadn't. The need to forgive ourselves lives in all of us.

Forgiveness is a manner of feeling and doing. If there is something you think you just cannot forgive yourself for, or something that you are having a hard time letting go of and forgiving yourself, do the following:

Write a letter to yourself, describing your hurt, love, anger, etc. Be completely honest and admit the happening and the need to forgive you. Read this letter aloud at least once and then burn this letter and take the ashes and immediately bury them in your yard or garden. Whenever you think of this, remind yourself that you have done ceremony to let it go, to forgive yourself. Then go on with your life. And don't worry, if there is something you wish you hadn't done, you will no doubt create the opportunity to "not do it" one more time.

When you truly have forgiven yourself, you no longer try to be a victim or punish yourself or cause others to punish you. Remember, unresolved personal issues can transform into cancer and other forms of disease.

Forgive yourself. You needed the experiences. Stay strong.

Notes ☀ Thoughts ☾ Prayers

Week Three

Death is never without purpose.

We all must die. This is a given in our lifetime. Once we have traveled our paths on this earth, it is time to move on. In completing our purposes, some live to be over a hundred, some leave in youth, some are aborted before they can develop, some never make it totally to this realm, and some come to this realm already lifeless. Only Spirit can know the number of destined hours during incarnations on this earth.

There are different realms to which a deceased's spirit can travel. This depends entirely on the person's purpose, the state of mind when dying, the desire and willingness to grow spiritually, and what one is taking from this realm that no longer needs to be here, whether it be emotional, physical, spiritual or mental. We all are destined to make this realm a better place by leaving and taking something with us. How we choose to accept this is personal.

Some of us will take a genetic code that is no longer needed in the familial line. Some will take anger, hate, and fear that others can no longer tolerate or learn from. Even babies take with them whatever blocks their parents from becoming better spiritual beings. All death is necessary and therefore we should not judge others in fulfilling the desires of Spirit. Just as we are not capable of understanding true love, we are not capable of understanding all aspects of death.

Stay strong and pray for deeper understandings of death.

Notes ☀ Thoughts ☾ Prayers

Week Four

Is it true that time heals all wounds, or if we let enough time pass, we learn to accept the ambivalent nature of others?

How often are we disappointed by the actions of others? How often do we say "if that person would just... things would be so much easier for me?" Humans have ambivalent natures and often do what they want to do, instead of what others expect of them. Frequently, people do not know why they do the things they do, other than it felt "like the right thing to do at the time." Waiting on discovering the purposeful reasoning behind things that hurt us can seemingly take forever when we cannot accept the happening in good faith. Perchance we are not meant to know all reasoning. Perhaps it is better to accept that others have their own agendas, just as we do. Whatever we feel wounded from today will eventually show us that Spirit had something much better planned for all involved.

When we are wounded and disappointed, we often complain, point fingers, spit out angry words, or even revel in being a victim. We are no longer children. We cannot continue to act as such. Do not wish harm upon those who disappoint you unless you want to experience the harm yourself.

Consider your own agenda and consider acceptance of what you cannot change while staying strong.

Notes ☀ Thoughts ☾ Prayers

January February
March April
May June
July August
September October
November December

Week One

Sacrifice cleanses the spirit.

What does sacrifice mean to you? Giving away something you really want to keep? Working hard in order to advance? Giving an offering to Spirit? Letting others take advantage of you because you care for them?

Sacrifice can be a double-edged sword if we are not sure of our intent. When we give something away, it does come back to us, but not necessarily from the person we give to. A great spiritual law is "what goes around, comes around." This includes bad as well as good. We get from life what we give. Whether we give love to others, or hate, it comes back to us.

When we truly care for another, we must remember: Caring deeply does not mean total sacrifice of one's beliefs. Caring deeply means listening to another's heart and considering the breaks. If we give ourselves totally to another, we are not honoring ourselves. There must be a spiritual boundary. A boundary that separates us from others so that we do not let anyone take advantage of us, or so that we do not take advantage of others. In relationships, sacrifice means keeping your connection to Spirit stronger than meshing with another. Sacrifice of this sort cleanses our spirits and keeps us focused with clarity on what is right for ourselves as well as others. No one wants to be smothered by caring. We all want to be respected.

Keep in mind that Spirit knows of what your spirit needs cleansing. Be willing to make the sacrifices. Stay strong.

Notes ☼ Thoughts ☾ Prayers

Week Two

Look underneath the dry hostility to find the painful truths.

How many of us have judged others because of abortions, spousal abuse, adultery, or sexual preference? How many of us have condemned those who do what we either have done, have considered doing, or are afraid we might do? If we examine our judgments of others, our so-called "holier than thou" attitudes, our indifference, our intolerance, and our belief that we are right and others are wrong, we will see that we are no better than those we condemn. Not a one of us is perfect, nor will we ever reach perfection.

There is evil at work in this world, but that is not relevant here. The point is that we at times put others down so that we might feel better than, or more religious, or more intellectual. Granted there are some people we do not need to be around because of personal reasons, but there are those we avoid because we do not understand how they view the world. We often fear what we do not understand. Have you had to make a painful decision that altered the future of others as well as your future? Have you considered that everyone on this planet is faced with the same type of decisions? Do you let your religion do your thinking for you when it comes to accepting others, or do you take time to consider you do not know all components surrounding another's actions?

Become more understanding of the actions of others
by realizing we can never know what is hidden
in the soul of another. Stay strong.

Notes ☼ Thoughts ☾ Prayers

Week Three

*Whatever you feel is dragging you down
is simply trying to get your attention.*

If living is painful to you, it is time to rethink your path. Do you dread going to work? Do you feel you are not helping others in any way? Do you think that you could be more productive in another area? If so, it is time to do what you came to this life to do. Time to search your heart and find what it is you should be doing. Time to live instead of exist.

Following one's true path does not mean all is well, or that life is abundant and easy. It means you will often question yourself, your actions, what Spirit tells you to do, and test yourself over and over to see if you are really "walking your talk." But it also means that you will feel rewarded in ways you never expected. This could be a simple thank you, a card, an email, or another form of clarification that what you do helps others along their paths. We all need to be reminded occasionally that we are doing what we came here to do, whether it is cleaning houses, setting broken bones, or giving strangers smiles to brighten their days.

Our existence is a constant dance of movement, change, molding, melting and remolding. Try to accept this.
Stay strong.

Notes ☀ Thoughts ☾ Prayers

Week Four

What is war? How can we define this frightening word?

What comes to mind when you think of war? Previous and present administrations have tried to desensitize us by commercializing war. We see pictures of women killed in arenas for mere infractions, children torn apart with flies circling their wounds, young men and women returning from battles in wheelchairs or in coffins. Realistic computerized war games, which turn murder into an amusing pastime, are available at the touch of a switch. We are bombarded with this imagery so often that many have to go deep into themselves to grasp compassion. Looking back over the past two thousand years, it is obvious that many wars were fought (and continue to be) because of religious and/or political imperialism. One group believes its ideology to be superior to another's. Regardless of causes, war disrupts the harmony of the world.

Make an attempt to go past the nonverbal consent caused by desensitization, to reawaken and bring to the surface the innate realization that we are all involved in the historical and recent events concerning war; that no one is insulated from these issues; that everyone has experienced the realities of war in some way. Then try to accept how blessed you are, regardless of what you may be going through.

Remember all who have been or still are engaged in war.
Stay strong.

Notes ☀ Thoughts ☾ Prayers

January February
March April
May June
July August
September October
November December

Week One

Some cannot deal with all their fears and regretful actions in this realm. Instead they take the most painful ones to the other realm and work to understand them there.

We all have to make decisions that we feel are the best at the time: Some for sacrifice, some to better ourselves or to hide our inadequacies, even some to stay out of more trouble. Making all the choices we are faced with in this life is not easy. Even those who have killed during war have to deal with the fact that they are murderers.

Do we ever really know Spirit's clear will for us? Do we take into consideration that we are responsible for our actions? Do we realize that responsibility really means the ability to respond? Many times we have been forced to made decisions for which we were not ready to respond. Life is not easy.

Many of us choose to try and deal with our choices and decisions. We ask for forgiveness, we give forgiveness to others and ourselves, and we make amends. But there are many who do not have the clarity, the ability, the willingness, the opportunity, or the courage to deal with all their actions. So when they pass over, they take their burdens and work with them in the other realm.

Don't worry about your loved ones never dealing with all their demons. We all are given ample opportunities to do so, in this life and the next. Stay strong.

Notes ☼ Thoughts ☾ Prayers

Week Two

The Universal Soul speaks from silence.

Out of the silence came our world, our existence, and our reality. We cannot hear this silence; we have to *listen to* this silence.

How hard it is to spend time in silence? Do you turn off the television, computer, radio, your mind often enough to understand what nourishment you can receive when you are being instead of doing? Are you uncomfortable just sitting in silence? How long does it take to quiet your thoughts, your fears, your desire to be in total control? Can you understand the language of the wind? Can you feel the heartbeats of trees? Can you remember the last time you felt totally at peace? At one with the entire universe? Do flowers ever smile at you?

We have to slow down long enough to realize all we have is this very moment. To understand that we cannot be of any use to anyone or ourselves if we don't take time to breathe in the creation of silence. Do you have a favorite tree to sit next to? A favorite body of water to walk by? A sacred place in your house for visiting the silence? If not, it is time to bring these into your life. To inhale and exhale the strength and worthiness of silence. How can you know where you are going if you do not know from whence you come? Soak in the silence with your whole being. Don't try to make sense of it, just allow it to fill every bit of your body, your mind, and your soul.

Listen to what is not being said. Stay Strong.

Notes ☼ Thoughts ☾ Prayers

Week Three

Creativity is a gift from Spirit to all humans.

Creativity calls to us from a deep inner recess where life and death are concurrently happening. It is a buffer to help us deal with life on life's terms. A way to connect to the Spirit of all things - a way to describe experiences that would otherwise be forgotten, or release the memories of experiences painful to remember but more painful to forget. A way to stop time, recapture time, crawl back into time, and even expel the idea of the existence of time altogether. It is a way for strangers to meet and merge in that mystic realm of otherworldly things, then leave one another, go on with their individual lives, untouched other than in spirit.

Creativity is Spirit seeking us through the medium of words, art, dance, music and so on. Of course the ultimate spiritual experience is beyond human comprehension, but to attempt this experience is why poetry, art, music, dance and so on exist.

Creativity is a metaphor for the universe's dreaming, and creativity as ceremony is a transport to this dreaming. Allow yourself to experience this other side of beyond by becoming more creative and immersing your soul in the creations of others. If Spirit is the source of creation, why can't creativity lead you back to the source?

Use creativity to enlighten and enrich your life and deepen your universal connection. Stay strong.

Notes ☀ Thoughts ☾ Prayers

Week Four

There is no magic in Spiritual medicine, or in being a Spiritual healer. How does anyone deal with such responsibility? There is no right or wrong answer, simply this question that melts away from the healer's consciousness as he or she becomes fully accepting of the accountability.

Being a true Spiritual healer has nothing to do with indulgence in religion but is centered on a relationship with Spirit. A true Spiritual healer is willing to be stripped to his/her bare inner self, to allow one's connection to Spirit to be questioned, to waver at times, and to know, above all other knowing, that one has no choice in the matter. Carrying Spiritual medicine is not a glorious accomplishment and has nothing to do with "honor" or "status" or even material goods. It means self-sacrifice and an often lonely soul and proper use of ego. Carrying medicine means the only way to build self respect is through a relationship with Spirit. All else is temporary and can be taken or given away at any time, at any whim of Spirit.

Carrying Spiritual medicine means dealing with people who are hurting, confused, sorry, lonely, non-caring, and sometimes just plain mean. It means being constantly humbled, and knowing and accepting that not everyone can or will heal. Medicine only opens the wound; Spirit does the healing when and if desired. Unseen forces made the choice for true Spiritual healers long ago.

If you are a Spiritual healer, or if you know one, remember that all are vessels only. Stay strong.

Notes ☀ Thoughts ☾ Prayers

January February

March April

May June

July August

September October

November December

Week One

*Light brings destruction to what has lived inside
the darkness for too, too long.*

We are multifaceted beings: physical, emotional, spiritual, and mental. We become aware of what we need to deal with, what learned actions cause others and us emotional pain. We seek help, get counseling, talk about it openly, and make a conscious effort to better ourselves. Then we become physically ill. We throw up. We are bed ridden. Once we become aware of what thoughts, actions-whatever we need to expel from our lives-after we have begun the work, our bodies help us to release the energy by cleansing, by bringing all from the darkness into the light. Our bodies store what we have experienced, whether it be trauma, regret of actions, or abuse. Once we have consciously brought it all to the surface, once our psyches are dealing with the issue, our bodies need to release what has been stored.

Spiritual cleansing awakenings do not happen overnight. It may seem that you wake one morning, and what you have been dealing with has finally been resolved in all your being. But this is all due to hard work, persistence, determination and the willingness to heal. Healing is a process. We have to realize we are to be involved in our spiritual growth, our spiritual awakenings. We have to cleanse all the residue.

Life is a mixture of sweet rain and rotten leaves.
Stay strong.

Notes ☀ Thoughts ☾ Prayers

Week Two

*Grief of losing a love one can stay within us for years.
Learning how to deal with it can be the answer
to moving toward acceptance.*

There are many ways to grieve. Some drink to take away the pain, some work harder, some lie, some cheat, some hurt emotionally day after day. Some blame the world as being against them. All of these are band-aids that never let the open wound breathe and heal. True grieving requires a method of honesty. Ignoring what is going on inside our psyches can be damaging to our spiritual growth. Pretending we do not care when we do, arguing for no apparent reason, blaming others instead of taking responsibility for our own feelings, and seeking pity for ourselves can cause no end of distress. Losing someone dear to you is painful, whether expected or not. Losing a pet can hurt as deeply as losing a loved one. But if we change our thinking from losing to acceptance of the cycle of life, we can heal more deeply.

Crying is an excellent way of grieving. Talking with someone, whether it is a close friend, family member, or therapist, can help as well. Do not hold on to grief and wear it like a badge. Let others know how you feel but do not seek pity. If you receive too much pity, you can learn to expect it and that is not good. Know that every person has a number of days in this life and when those days are filled, it is time to move on. Do not hold on to grief. Do not let it overtake your soul.

Pray to be shown how to move toward acceptance. Stay strong.

Notes ☀ Thoughts ☾ Prayers

Week Three

Crows are our buddies.

We have many stories and dances referring to the importance of animal speak and celebration of their existence. We know that animals are a part of creation as much as we are. Animals are teachers. Indigenous healers have long known that observing sick animals can lead them to medicinal plants. This is the language of Spirit.

Can you recall a special experience you have had with an animal, bird, or fish? Perhaps you've heard the bone-chilling howl of a wolf, or come face-to-face with one. Maybe you've been blessed to hear the mysterious caws of crows reminding you that you are never alone in your thoughts. Or, perhaps while riding a horse, you realized you and the animal became one spirit for a while. Did dolphins ever warn you that you had swam too far out from the ocean shore? Or maybe your memory is of your pet, lying next to you, cuddling you in a time of stress.

These are primordial experiences that go beyond words. They are evidence of the spiritual interconnectedness of all things. A connection that removes us from the world of logic and connects us to our inner nature. A necessary connection in order to live life deeply. Animals have unique abilities that we humans have to develop through creative thinking and by honoring them. By observing and respecting animals, deep lessons can be learned.

Don't forget to feed the crows. Stay strong.

Notes ☀ Thoughts ☾ Prayers

Week Four

Spirit beings are all around us.

The universe is complex, of this there is no doubt. However, there are natural and spiritual laws that remain true, regardless of who experiences them. This is not to say that humans hold all the answers to the mysteries of the world; this is not possible at this stage of the human race. But many of us do believe in the mysteries of the universe, even if they cannot be "proved" mathematically or scientifically.

There are spirit beings who help us, who guide us, and there are spirit beings who can confuse us as well. Whenever you feel the presence of a spirit, always ask if this spirit is from the Light. If you feel it is not, then ask it to leave. Tell it to go toward the Light so that it can become cleansed. Some deceased souls do not know they are dead and they cling to people, places, and things they recognize. We can help them by asking them to go to the Light, so that they will no longer be stuck in this realm.

Spirit beings are all around us at any given moment. We just have to be open to this fact and pay attention when we feel a sudden coldness envelop us, feel a playful touch on our hair, hear a familiar song in our minds, or smell a certain aroma that reminds us of a loved one who has crossed over to the other realm. Just to feel their presence can give us solace in times of stress or fear. These spirits have their work to do in helping us, so they need us as much as we need them.

Be responsive. Stay strong.

Notes ☀ Thoughts ☾ Prayers

January February
March April
May June
July August
September October
November **December**

Week One

You've struggled far too long over empty nests.
When one is empty, take apart and begin anew.

Isn't it time to let go of that so-called dream that has turned into a nightmare? Time to realize that if something is meant to be, it will be, and if not, there is not a thing you can do to make it happen? Why do we hold on to what we know we shouldn't? Long after the nest is empty, long after the wind and rain has changed the nest into something unrecognizable? Is it because we are stubborn, or afraid that if we let go, we might lose control? Not get what we want? Get what we want and then realize we don't want it?

We are such obstinate beings when it comes to hanging on, clinging to what we know we shouldn't, acting as if we don't care instead of feeling the loss so that we can get on with our lives; so that we can begin anew.

Whether a relationship, a piece of clothing, a creation, a job, or something we don't even want to talk about anymore, when it is time to let go, we intuitively know it. And when we know it and don't let go, Spirit will remind us in ways that can hurt. Then, if we still don't let go, Spirit will step in and make us let go. Nothing new can come into our lives as long as we are squeezing the crap out of something we need to let go of. How do you know when you have finally let go? When the outcome no longer matters.

One of the greatest offerings of intuition is knowing when to let go. Pay attention, and act on the knowing. Stay strong.

Notes ☀ Thoughts ☾ Prayers

Week Two

Whatever the next story in your life is,
it will come to you; it will find you.

Our individual lives are a story unfolding, day-by-day, revelation-by-revelation, and creation-by-creation. Our stories are energies manifested through our decisions, paths, acceptances, refusals, and choices. We are all connected, but are unique in what our storied lives entail.

Our ancestors have left unfinished business and we have the opportunity to finish it, or leave it for the next generation. We have blood memories and we have the choice to bring these memories to the surface and experience them if we so desire. Some people choose to do this through hypnosis, some through meditation, some through massage, and some through past life exploration. Our past lives co-mingle forming such an entanglement that it is hard to rifle through everything during one lifetime.

If you feel stuck, held back by stress, afraid of what is coming next, remember that life unfolds as it supposed to. We cannot rush anything that is not ready to come to fruition. And worrying does us no good at all, even though it seems it has become a national pastime for many. Worry is what tries to bend the river and pull down the moon. The infusing spirit of all things, the interconnecting invisible web, spins itself continuously, creating though us. If we can learn to trust this process, our next story will arrive right on schedule.

Know that your life unfolds as it is supposed to. Stay strong.

Notes ☼ Thoughts ☾ Prayers

Week Three

You are strong only when you can recognize and accept your weaknesses so that they may not be used against you.

Realize you are a human being having a spiritual experience. Realize you are not perfect. Realize you did not come to this life to attain perfection. There is nothing more beautiful than harmony and harmony means being at one with yourself, accepting all that makes you who you are.

If there is something you can do about your weaknesses do it. If not, acquaint yourself with them, be aware of them, so that others cannot "push your buttons" or use your weaknesses against you. Remember you are at your weakest when you pretend to be at your strongest. So how do you get stronger? Deal with the truth, regardless of how it makes you feel. Make amends to others you feel you have wronged, and don't forget yourself in the process.

If you are on the path of personal power only, you will create an imbalance in your system and cause destruction of yourself; you will slow the healing process and never feel completely at ease. Always consider your motives before your actions. Be grateful. Be good to yourself. Take time to sit in the silence. Spend time with animals. Do something for someone and remain anonymous in the doing or giving. And try your best to get along with those who drive you insane.

Stay strong.

Notes ☼ Thoughts ☽ Prayers

Week Four

The mysteries remain awaiting appreciation.

From various tribal creation stories to the Maya and Hopi declarations of the emergence of new worlds, Indigenous peoples have explanations of how this universe exists and evolves.

Indigenous people know that a spiritual force that cannot be destroyed connects everything. All is Spiritual energy and relationships thereof.

We know that time and space are temporary, and that neither can exist until we recognize them. Our existence is a constant dance of movement, change, molding and melting and remolding. While in human form, our purpose is to grow spiritually, take care of the land, care for each other, and make sure our moments here are reflected appreciatively in all we do. When we circle back to death, our bodies return to the mountains, the trees, the water, back to our original DNA.

What defines a mystery for you? How you think of someone and then hear from that person? How you know when one of your loved ones needs help? How babies come from the merging of sexual energy? Energy makes up this universe. No doubt we are one of the greatest mysteries of all, and we are here to explore and accept whatever we need in order to make the most of our existence. We can celebrate mysteries even though we cannot fully understand them.

Be grateful for all mysteries. Stay strong.

Notes ☀ Thoughts ☾ Prayers

About the Author

MariJo Moore, of Cherokee, Irish and Dutch ancestry is an author/ artist/ poet/ essayist/ lecturer/ editor/ anthologist/ publisher/ workshop presenter/ psychic/medium.

The recipient of numerous literary and business awards, she is the author of over a dozen books including *The Diamond Doorknob* and *When the Dead Dream* (two novels of which she is currently writing a screenplay), *Confessions of a Madwoman, The Boy With a Tree Growing From His Ear and Other Stories*, and *Spirit Voices of Bones*. She is also editor of various anthologies including *Genocide of the Mind: New Native Writing*, and *Birthed From Scorched Hearts: Women Respond to War*. She resides in the mountains of western North Carolina.

For information on ordering books, scheduling a consultation, or hosting a workshop, go to www.marijomoore.com.

Drawings of the Author